GHOST APPLES

GHOST APPLES

poems

Katharine Coles

Red Hen Press | *Pasadena, CA*

Book design by Tansica Sunkamaneevongse

Library of Congress Cataloging-in-Publication Data

Names: Coles, Katharine, author.
Title: Ghost apples: poems / Katharine Coles.
Description: First edition. | Pasadena, CA: Red Hen Press, [2023]
Identifiers: LCCN 2022027677 (print) | LCCN 2022027678 (ebook) | ISBN
   9781636280844 (paperback) | ISBN 9781636280851 (ebook)
Subjects: LCGFT: Poetry.
Classification: LCC PS3553.O47455 G48 2023 (print) | LCC PS3553.O47455
   (ebook) | DDC 811/.54—dc23/eng/20220613
LC record available at https://lccn.loc.gov/2022027677
LC ebook record available at https://lccn.loc.gov/2022027678

The National Endowment for the Arts, the Los Angeles County Arts Commission, the Ahmanson Foundation, the Dwight Stuart Youth Fund, the Max Factor Family Foundation, the Pasadena Tournament of Roses Foundation, the Pasadena Arts & Culture Commission and the City of Pasadena Cultural Affairs Division, the City of Los Angeles Department of Cultural Affairs, the Audrey & Sydney Irmas Charitable Foundation, the Meta & George Rosenberg Foundation, the Albert and Elaine Borchard Foundation, the Adams Family Foundation, Amazon Literary Partnership, the Sam Francis Foundation, and the Mara W. Breech Foundation partially support Red Hen Press.

First Edition
Published by Red Hen Press
www.redhen.org

For Joan Link Coles
1932–2022
Again and for the last time

[F]or me [the word] "portrait" fails to convey
the emotions portrayed in art inspired by a person.
Or an animal.
  —Samantha Peale

CONTENTS

ANIMAL

IF THE OLDER I GET THE LESS I KNOW

WON'T WAIT

ANIMAL

LIVING WILD,

not being. *Beauty is*
a defiance of authority, feral
A falling back into arms
I trust, returning to something not

The same thing. Fetching,
I incline to fleece and flannel, raise
Myself each morning and feel
Flight in daylight, flight refining

Stars or meteors, body not defined
One way. What ruffles
Feathers, what my mind? If I prowl
Free among trees and grasses

Or traversing the pavements,
I am the catch.

LONG VIEW

Back when I wondered what
I had to do, I knew
I would know it when I saw it,
The way I would know a lion

Flicking her tail in the grass had
Fixed her desire on me. Back then
Each day opened itself, brilliant
And blank as empty glass. This

I knew of beauty: its hunger,
Its delicate provocations. And yes,
I believed the day waited to be filled,
And me to fill it. Only how

Would I ever open myself so far,
How could I pour without spilling?

ANIMAL

One can die. This
Numinous skin. The way

Flesh becomes everything
And everything around it

Taken in. Including all
It's not but may anticipate

Or imagine. Including drag
Its belly; including perform

A hundred push-ups on a rock
And sun shining, all in

A day's work, and
Curling up at day's end into

A ball of self, under a leaf
Or thicket of softest green,

Waking again noticing
The sun has risen, not

Another day keeps
Coming up new, going by.

WHEN

I looked like a tufty
Someone would want to hold
Between his palms to stroke
Or squeeze because I kept

My claws retracted and my teeth
Looked small and milky between
Lips half opened. I let them
Pet me sometimes, what else

Could I do, and think my body
Was made for them though it had
Nothing to do with me. That
Was then. Now the lip's

Upward curve, the fingers
Opened: do you see
Smile or snarl, invitation,
A paw beginning its swipe? You

Figure it out. I'm done helping,
Quieting, sending my mind
Anywhere else while
You take me in hand.

SICK OF GRIEF—

especially mine. Look outside,
Look in: our Henri whistles up
His flock across a jungle

And I answer. One will
Outlive the other and song
Continue. We love where we are
Loved. We don't nest in treetops

Of course: ceilings and floors
Divide us, staircases and doors
Open up and through, you know
What I mean. If not, imagine

A small bird in the window,
Fanning open green and yellow
Wings for me to admire, green leaves
Dazzling, yellow sun come on.

SMALL SONG

I have a ghost at my shoulder. I wear
His heart on my sleeve. I keep

Him to hand and fold his wings
Under my ribs. He calls, his voice

A sharp green shadow, voice a scarlet
Blazon through the trees

Which branch and crown in us
And rustle gently in the breeze.

WAKE

Eleven finches branch a line
And twitter in order, others I thought
Were leaves popping up from

The treetops, wind-flicked, looking out
The feeders I bring in at dusk
Against the raccoons. Each dawn

I put them out again, having
Risen to impatiences of birds
A-twitch, finches and their singing

Kind, sparrows et al., and also
Orioles clicking out territories,
Tanagers, grosbeaks, tiny

Hummingbirds buzzing
My head, angry at my lassitude,
Considering not gratitude,

Only hunger. What pace do
I get up to, I ask myself, pulling
Robe close, and for whom? No

Point wondering, I know, except
Wondering gives my mind
One more thing to charm it.

BIRD

Appear as hovercraft,
Smoke and mirrors

Vanishing into air, but feel
Yourself as gristle

And keratin, sinew, barb,
Bone. To rise takes

All the power you can
Muster, more work than

Running yourself into
Heart and breath, more even

Than sleep. A body can't rest
On the invisible, must

Twist and shift, muscle draft
And current, wind strafing

The eyes. However you make
It look effortless, do not

Deceive yourself flight
Sets you free. Want it

Anyway, air above
And beneath, lifting hard.

BEE

All summer I buzz, I depart
And return. My body knows where
Dandelions release their nectar,
And, later, marjoram.

Who are you to tell me what
Memory is, what's to come?
I carry desire in my legs, pockets
Aglow. I dwell not upon

The future, but in it. All my
Going and coming prepares
The world to slow. Soon,
The sealing of the hive,

Then, settling, my body will rev
Its furnace. Then winter.

CRICKET

Seventeen degrees and in
The greenhouse off our bedroom

Tunes a machine, little sex
-engine, pistons pumping

Seduction though no
Being but us will hear. Whatever

We may call it, this is
Not singing. We too woo

Out of time, not early
But late. While cold deepens

We work our thighs for comfort.
Let our song deceive us.

SEVEN (or so) POSES

Who poses, the woman
Or the crane, the woman or
The buffalo looking as if he wears
A tiger for a skin. Two swans

Or the woman, the woman
Or history, the girl almost
Woman or her nearest
Attachment, also almost—

Or her dream. The dream
Dances, faint and whimsical,
Neither woman nor girl

Nor in between. He leads
A dog-sized cricket on a string,
The cricket also posing.

MAGNOLIA

Fossil flowers bloom prehistory
Into such glowing even
Pollen bearers express iridescent

Age, how 25 million years ago
Insects hadn't yet taken wing, so
Could only climb. And lovely,

The beetles' small green shine
Reflecting a garden where
Everything is green, budding

Before leaf. How leathery
The flowers must be, to survive
Insect legs scrabbling. And swoon:

On the one hand, that burrowing;
Deep at heart, perfume.

GHOST APPLES

The ones we ate
We shouldn't have

Yet. The ones we imagined
Eating. The ones we left

Too long on the bough until
The rain froze around them

And they slipped out
The bottom, leaving behind

Perfect crystal shapes: present
And absent, clear

Mysteries, bodies made
Transparent vessels of the sun

And, in the sun, their own
Soft robes vanishing light.

Like anyone, I'd rather go
Around in my own skin. And yet

We don't. Once I bit
An apple. It bit me back.

PASSETH

The apple doesn't come from nowhere,
Or for that matter anywhere, and the tree

Also counts its days. Or counteth,

As the case may be, enumeration
Elevated by grammar and the world

Filling itself with never-

Enough jokes. How many sunrises
Since last frost? How many to go until

It's safe to let loose, statistically

Speaking? The trees want their blossoms'
There-and-gone unfoldings

Not to freeze. Want to pull

Water through their fibers into what
Transpires and make sunlight raw

Material. Don't we all want to feel

Fingertips plump into fruit? If this turn
Strikes you as fanciful, don't think

So much. Only palms-full. Only

Sweetness filling your hands then
Too muchness you count on, recount

As night lengthens and its shiver takes you.

NIGHT JAR

Sometimes like everyone I prefer
Sleeping. That simple, however

Extravagantly Keats put it: to cease
And then what? Truth

Is, and we all know it, there is no
"No pain" for us, and when it comes

Down to it, who wants to fade, even so
Lyrically? Best to go

Chirring, however
Discordant, however I grow

Bored with my own self, though
Also I may find delight

Racketing into the dark
Bower. Or, without ceasing, fly.

PELICAN TAKES MY HAND

for a fish leaping, and later
I have to ask who

Owns what, when
What won't let go? We've all

Made error out of hunger
Over our heads. Now gulp,

Repeat: hurricane churning
Offshore doesn't

Drown, not swell nor sea
But panic, the body

Forgetting itself how
It breathes not water

But air. In the moment
Bird lets go to catch

Its own breath, and
Again, and finds it

Gone. Later, regrets
The one that got away. Or

Let go becomes *Okay,*
Forget, move on.

THE MIND MANAGES ITSELF

or minds itself in all
Its crazy senses, so today

Not watching the time
I mind what I will

Eat with friends this evening,
Textures my tongue already

Mulls over, taste being
A form of imagination. So

Much of our talk these days
Returns to meat: always

Thinking. We worry
We are electrified

Water and salt, mineral
Scatterings; it all adds up

To something we occupy but
Barely grasp. Shall I

Eat others situated likewise,
As I may, and if not where

Does kinship end
And at what, and when

Therefore wield I my fork, given
Fish so deep they fashion

Tools and dig; when
Should I pick up my knife

And set its teeth
Biting, given mother-

liness of trees, their underground
Chatter, their historical

Accuracy and canniness? So
Clam and carrot

Become me. And those
Trees, still a-racketing, also

Burst into leaf. I hunger for
Green, really myself, not

Knowing as usual. We keep
Thunking along, our bodies

Lost in thought, minds feeding
Always with others. Salt, oh,

Salt on the tongue, I am
Forever chewing things over.

WORM

     1.   It works its way through the canopy.
Leaf by leaf, it ruminates
On what its body makes. Trees chew over
News and light, muttering, but the leaf

Can't escape. If it thinks, the leaf imagines
Being chewed apart, dismember-
ment enacted, routine. How to shrug off,
How repel. Above deep shade emanates

Blue and dazzle, but neither
Leaf nor caterpillar knows a thing about
Light's scattering—or do they?—or that

When I take to the tops of trees
I want to fly but fall. Beneath,
They occupy themselves: caterpillar, leaf

2. It consumes in time. Why should they
Be different than we are in this way,
Each selved, absorbed, at work. The caterpillar
Might turn into a metaphor for whatever

Grows and eats, whatever rustles,
And fights the other off, or fails, but
It remains itself, stubborn. Metaphor
Extends itself or sticks it to us

While we grieve the body, our minds
Consumed with it. We feed
Ourselves, on ourselves. This morning
And every morning I clean my teeth,

Preparing them, failing, becoming
Already part of the feast.

WORRY

More fussed about disappointing the world
Than it about me. That's

The way of things and therefore
How they go. All that said, doesn't the world

Glitter and gleam, don't trees shake their manes
And the lion never lie down. Oh, lamb, why

Should the world worry? The world
Can't fail, no matter what we do.

TILT

Canberra, September

So long as giddy light sweeps along down

The hillside, I walk
At odds with time's

Gusts and fidgets, how what it takes to settle

Takes time to un-
Settle, a startle

Or start, my unruly heart arrested when a flock kicks

Up on the field—seven
Kangaroos—leaping

Ta-da with my pulse. A *mob*, I remember, ordinary, so

Unlike any creature
I know, I forget I pull

Loose under this sky there is nothing beyond

But fire, emptiness
Wildly bodied, heaven

Mapping a new way as lights come on below, plotting

The valley's contours
And guiding me, now

Twilight falls and like all paths this one bends itself

Under the woods. *Don't*
Walk after dark

Stories teach us, and a nice woman whispers, *All*

Snakes are poison
But the blind snake. Won't

The others see me then, and aren't snakes cold-

Blooded and torpid, spring
Not yet here? Thus time

Quarrels with itself: equinox coming, a season

Gone, and I look on
The bright side, days

Lengthening and the sun glowing almost warm, though

My own house
Slides down darkness

Into ice. So distant, the future barreling past—not

An idea but
Thrill in the blood

I try to attach to a sky plumbing space as plumbs

My sky, to gum trees
Draped with birdcalls

I don't know, and cockatoo grazing in herds, popping up

Heads like so many
Conventioneers. I should

Say *pandemoniums*. A cockatoo chews no cud, chuckles

Rather than lows, is common
As squirrels I hardly

Notice back home, and I work to remember my own landscape

Is also shadowed,
Haunted and slo-mo

Adrift, geologically speaking. No wonder I lose

Myself, knowing
Beyond the chill blue

Orbs rough and tumble into the end of time. True,

Nobody chooses to be
A stranger. But look.

Who on earth would choose to stay put.

NOISY BIRDS

Anything but melodic, from the trees
They cacophone in Australian, making me
Want to pin them down, to name
Their othering. They sound more

Annoyed than symphonic, not
Talking about me, but about
What lives in bark and weed, fat
Grubs waiting to be winkled,

Fruit and ripening seed, that bird
Just over there who may be
Ready at last to woo
Or be wooed. The females

Make the decisions about that
Sort of thing, despite the usual male
Postures and clumsy rushes
The females disregard. And when

Their mates go foraging, the females
Look for a little something
Extra, if you know what I mean. For now,
For all I can see, they masquerade

As leaves, or fly so fast they blur,
Or vanish into voice, as if it were
All their lives are worth. Some
Other woman might be tempted

To make sense, to formulate
A fable, or, worse, an allegory—

Birds, noise, who can or can't
Be seen or might be listening

Or ticked off, I've let things
Tend that way—but that would be
Too easy. In real life, a stranger
Crosses grass under trees, being

Her human body, desiring
Just a glimpse, their
Own swift beings making
All the noise they need.

WHISTLER

I might have married a painter,
Therefore his mother. A radar

Detector, a snow-covered
Mountain, a novel

By John Grisham not even
Out yet. No, I wed

The cop directing my rush,
Toot toot, a trainer to test

Agility, a kettle calling
Time to steep. Yes,

But I married this bird you must
Close your eyes to know

At scale, to hear his trills
And fancy arpeggios

Come-come-hithering.
His note of warning.

PET NAMES

Salt and what
We bring to it, parts

We've spent the day mostly
Not thinking of, the ones

We name for animals, sparrow-
Like birds or birds

Of a feather who can't
Not crow. Despite the joke

He's always the one
Who introduces fish into

The equation: forgive me, but
A puss that hasn't been

Fed or stroked smells
Only like itself.

LEDA

Whatever you've heard,
I wouldn't let myself

Say I was taken in, by
Or on a ride, for

A fool. I could take on
But prefer opening

My wings to being
Carried, shaking my tail, flying

All that high when
You release me.

IF THE MIND FEARS FREEDOM

Give it a box. Live in,
Live out. The eyes see both ways

And at the window, the young towhee
Keeps trying to get to the stranger

Who almost meets him in the glass,
Their beak and claws clicking.

He's been at it all summer, now
Turning August, turning heat to fall.

WHALE FALL

Because they live in the dark
Mostly they live in

Their ears, listening, singing
Back. We drop microphones

And eavesdrop below
The surface, letting them make us

Fishers of sound. They surface
When they want and bob

Pointing their eyes at us in our
Strange vessels and bright

Flotation vests. Why don't we
Come on in? They flip and dive

And return, great tempt
-resses, and wink, and finally

When they've exhausted
Our capacity to amuse them

Roll their vastness into
Greater vastness. Because

They sometimes throw
Themselves onto our shores,

Enormous, evacuated, where
They never meant to be, and like

Any body stink, we think
We know their fates. But when

They come to their ends in deep
Waters, like us alone, they sink

Back to where they came from
Out of sight and deep, where

We all came from, whether
Or not we end there.

YOU WON'T FIND CONSOLATION

or. The deer, nearly
Colorblind, see blue

Better than we do, more
Blue than we know, a blue

I am not consoled
Lives beyond me. Imagine

Their sky, saturated, how
Do they bear it, and

The alpine lake where
They drink in summer, glacier-

Fed, reflecting back it all back
Plus. Consider

The glacier, blue at heart deep-
Frozen for millennia, blue

Its core and vanishing
In your lifetime. A rush,

A trickle, this is how
It goes? Around the lake,

Boulders harden themselves.
Green firs. And there, a perfect

Center, the lake's clear,
Unreadable eye.

IF THE OLDER I GET
THE LESS I KNOW

IF THE OLDER I GET THE LESS I KNOW—

1.

—the more I wonder, What the hell
Is anyone talking about? We all knew
At eighteen and the young still do:
Les femmes d'un certain age have gone

Soft over napping and staring
At the window, as if things
We've lost might flutter around
The feeders, fluffing their wings, singing

Forgotten names. What youngster
Would spend all her time with whatever
Those birds used to be called, and where are
My devices, style, sense of certainty? But

Oh, what we've gained, if once
We could remember what we call it.

2.

—the young know more, or
They did in my day. They read our signs
Sidelong as they sidle out the door,
If they even look our way,

And why should they,
Given our apparent gentleness, how
We no longer keep our skin in
The game. Back then, I don't recall

Pausing to hear a Townsend's solitaire
Sing from the leaves. Where hastening? Toodle
-oo or so, heading elsewhere.
Lookie: I've arrived, brimful of guile,

No more legible. Thanks, I'll keep my chair,
Little one. For now, I'll stay right here.

BREASTS

The minute I no longer care
How they keep themselves, and where,
They rise to sally forth at night, and
Next I know they've gone gung

-ho, twirling, full of themselves, all
Look here. I say, *Pipe down, will*
You: people are staring; I've earned
A little sleep at my age. *What age?* they

Say, *Good luck with that*, and haul
Off after whatever adventure they're
Onto, and the next. Firmly attached,

What can I do but follow? *Watch*
Yourselves, my friendlies, I say.
And, *Keep an eye out, old and young.*

TIME

You can change me with
A touch, too, but when I
Touch you change grows,
I can take it in hand.

Meanwhile, my mystery
Bodies forth into legend.
Nobody told me I hadn't
Use for beauty, that it

Wouldn't stick with me
Nor I by it. Now I live by wit
And carry my body lightly

As I may. How many years does
It take to change so
Much you can grow happy?

WIT

The ends I reach
Live in the dark
Heart of metaphor, twisting

And turning to find
A place at the center. How
I wish there were more

I might live by. With all
My soul wish mine
Were brief.

UNCANNY

The trinkets in my grandmother's
Keepsake box, their frayed

Ends of ribbons and quizzically
Carved faces, long gone

Jewels of paste and gilt—why not
Let them go, and what has

Become of the diamond
My grandfather put on her hand near

A century gone. How heavy
It got before she took it off. She

Pawned it of course, turning it in
-to that odd space of someone

Else's love, then she married another
Someone else, *anyone.* So

My brain haunts me, unfitting, igniting
Darkened pathways to bring

Back the dead; so Emily
Dickinson takes up space inside

Me, always rummaging, shining
Her flashlight around my sock drawers

And niches. Our old macaw
For example, was so

Resplendent in his feathered suit. Still
Present, he rests under primroses

Near the greenhouse door. When
He rests. When any of us do.

HANDS

Always something—too
Large for their wrists, fingernails
Tearing, unpolished—and then
Oz sends the photo: in one

A sheaf; in the other, a phone,
Also with poems, both luminous
Gestures from the dark, and above
My face in shadow, lips

Pursed around a word. My father,
Edging into his own dark
Downward spiral, took my fingers
And said, *They are beautiful, they are*

Your mother's. She was on
Her way to meet us, probably angry,
Also unknowing. Too late
Now, watching my hands stilled

In flight, I am taken
By new love for flaw
And ache: comfort all the same,
The current moment, not

Golden, unable to see itself
Clear. Now, what strength the body
Gathers to it, pleasures banked
And glowing against the night

And still burning itself out, especially
Lying here beside you, one
Or both of us sleeping, or
All hands awake.

GHOST HEART

In the lab scrub out its past
Life, make its matrix your own
Pure white rack to hang

Your shirt on, but remember the heart
Has to eat twenty-four seven, you know
How hungry it is, and its cells

Don't grow by themselves. Later
When the whole body moves
Past newness into the ordinary

And beyond and finally becomes
Its next self scattering, the heart's
Scaffold will also return not to its

Original body but, with yours
It has become, into whatever
Becomes you next. And that other

Mortal tatter, which fell into
The earth or rose as ash heartless
And so light on the air

It flies, will find yours, some
Small part of it, one particle
Then another passing.

INVISIBLE

Who knew I was bigger inside
-out, or where I might go
When I yank the heart from your sleeve
Then vanish. Inside my head

I become nothing
But space you can't see
The end of, so roomy
Every wall dissolves. Far now

Inside, I become all open
-aired, I float pavilions
And flocks of geese arrow
Overhead. Who knew speed

Could send so deep, who knew it
Would make this kind of racket?

LEAVING MIDDLE AGE

They cut off one leg and put it
Back. Then another. Then

Cut it off again. They pull out
An eye, return it. This time

Buckle it in. They find
Some piece missing

And replace it. Find an extra
Lump or wild hair, remove it,

Sand you down. Time takes
A parent, with a word estranges

A brother, old friend. Time moves
Houses, builds over landmarks

You navigate by, so you can't
Find the right road, the turn

You need to take. They
Expect you to be grateful, being

Rearranged this way, still
Just to remain. Having

Outlasted so many, so much
You will pull yourself

Together, get up happy
Enough, and go on.

TIME FLAWS

as does the world, and I mistake
Everything. Blades nick, glass slices,
Nails puncture, branches scratch.
So many things fracture

The body, force propelling any
Object into it, even mere gravity
Bringing the body's own weight
Down to break

Its fall. Ripening, any body
Damages itself inside out, so his
Which I love gives way what

It knitted out of mother's flesh
Out of air and food and water
Before it eats, in the end, its heart out.

ONE BODY

                      can't replace
Another, nor stand

in nor under
-study. Until I hate it

I love every last
Noise it makes.

MARRIAGE

A magnet. No, a leash. No,

It bites its own apple
Then spits. So many things

Itch me: a wasp, a feather,

An old sore spot. I could keep
My temper, I could lose it.

And I do, and I do.

BODIES AT 60

touch each other lightly then less
So. Take their time, lose
Track, absent

-mind themselves. They
Sleep like animals
Eat, animals trying

Anything once, rooting
Noses, going all in. Let us
Then celebrate night

-gowns or their absences,
Hail what we neglect
Settling as skin meant to

Keep us tears
And bruises, muscles
Fray, bones attenuate. Even

Now think what pleasure keeps
Giving: oil on the tongue,
Currents through dark places

Conducting pulses too
Deep to hear. Anything
But quiet. We cannot

Pull too much. Oh, wild
Hair, warp and wrinkle, down
-ward drift. Let's always

Love and pet them, love
And pet. Let's not
Ever put them down.

IN MY DREAM

Having forgotten my pajamas, I entertain
Revelation, always there. Gone
Friends pop in, long- or near-dead
Teachers yet professing—at least, their poems

Cloud the air, best-case scenario for poets
Embarked on that condition. You
Are all here, whether or not you know it
Or I do, all who still inhabit some

More-or-less-traveled pathway—though
A ghost might flash at any moment, who-
Who-ing desire, or fear. So what, if one
Demands my attention, if you deserve

Apologies or thanks—when you arrive
Looking for recognition, will I find it?

FACE OF AN ANGEL

Do you think he was ready?
Do you think he knew for days?
Do you think he'd had tea on the veranda
Or was he lounging in bed, had he been

There for days? If he knew
Do you think he minded
Or did he lounge around in bed, being
Fed red cherries out of season,

Do you think he minded
Paying the freight to bring
Red cherries out of season
To that island where no cherries grew?

He wouldn't have paid.
It wasn't the money to bring cherries
To that island where no cherries grew,
But every other fruit thrived—

No, it wasn't the money. To desire cherries
He had to look past guava and star fruit,
Every other fruit thriving,
Watered and tended with his own hand.

Guava and star fruit: looking beyond
Could he swallow tea on the veranda,
A little water, another hand to tend him?
Do you think he was ready?

ELEGY

She squared herself like a shirt box.
In her skull, a cat stretched.

She smoked all night, one then
The other, whisky lighting her way.

In daylight, how would she not
Die early? The cat inside her

Sharpened her claws. One thought
And another began, a swell in open ocean

Like all the swells you don't notice
Because they keep coming, that's

What the sea looks like. Who understood
Beauty's force as she did, for whom

Beauty was never a given? Who saw
Words make their meanings

At a distance, in sighs and ripples. In her
Angles the sea darkly glimmered, the sea

A cat who will never lie down, stretching
And curling while my friend stalked

Its shore watching, my friend
Who also will not lie down.

AFTER SUICIDE

Deprived of frozen ground, the hand shovel
He would in another time have bent
His back to, he turned the starter on his
Backhoe and drove it growling across

The cemetery lawn. He gouged
Tracks as he went, then tore out a hole
Bigger than a boy-sized soul or its blue
Satin-lined box could fill, still

Not large enough for rage
Everyone else called grief. This
I understand. Not suffering's method

But its size, its ragged edges
That can't be folded, can't be made
Tidy to hold, or small enough to name.

DREAM OF REFUGE

I have nothing to teach. My student's gone
There and back and I have never
Made it halfway. Meanwhile, I'm humping up
The steps to some church, its lord

Making me work to reach his house, one
God much like another. I've heard
I should keep my purse hidden
Until I reach the doors and pay to enter

But around me so many palms open
I imagine my student's flights, his close
Shaves, and dig for coins. Inside, more stairs
Wind into the sky and I rise

As if I have nothing better to do. Then
I reach the sky and find I haven't.

TIRED OF THE PRESENT,

                              I want the future
Sooner than, want the wind Earth
Generates in its turning to ruffle
My hair as before. This

Despite my years, which unaccountably
Won't stop adding, despite aches
Some mornings keeping me
From scaling the ridge where time

Blows its hardest, as if to sweep
All I know away. As I go
So goes the world, of course, how
Could I know better? Darling, for now

Of course I care, knowing all I am
I want, and you, though not sensibly.

SEVEN AT TABLE

Four drinking red, four
White will never
Add up. Talking about

Inexorability, building one
Event from another, the
She says and then he

Does of what occurs
And. Someone tried to
Break the chain, stepping right

While another zagged diag-
onally left and I watched you
Lift your glass, your legs

Crossed lightly, and levitate
Yourself on out of there.

CONFECTION

The most artful feels
Most honest. You can

Tell by the honesty
It seems to exude, the natural

Shape its edges sketch,
Meringue a perfect

Flourish of egg as if
It grew from air. Tell

Everything about it
And nothing but how

It vanishes inside you,
Taking you in.

KENSINGTON HIGH

An ordinary Thursday in July
I keep seeing brides

Not climbing registry steps
Or blooming out of church doors

Like peonies on fast-forward
But workaday as anyone

Trudging along pavements,
Their trains flung over

Their arms, veils smoking
Skyward, their heads

Blowing their tops. What
Are they all doing this day

Hot for London, mild for home,
Moving with steady purpose, faces

Bent to the pavers, burning
Up inside their icy confections?

Before them lies catastrophe
Or bliss, no way

I'll ever know, but if it's Thursday
It's Independence Day back home

And I would be celebrating,
If I were there, our imperfect union,

Celebrating even fireworks
And hot words, heeding not

The tanks rolling into the capitol,
Their purpose visible but unknown.

I TELL MYSELF

Stop complaining, or be taken
As a kind of woman—
Who knows—you
Who have loved mostly men

Mostly one at a time and feel
These days no obligation to love
The rest, or claim so, or even
To love them in aggregate,

Any more than you would all
Dogs or all babies, heaven
Forbid—must I repeat
Myself—before you have

The slightest idea what
One might get itself up to.

IF TRAGEDY UNFOLDS

                                    across
A single day, its cross written
Into the record, what of this

Lifetime whose end we insist on
Forgetting will come and is
Coming, even now we accept

Our daily portions and the sun
Passing its time bathes us
And we can't yet hear thunder

Cracking the horizon? What
Relief we will find in at last
Its breaking. Remember

Baptism is also always violence
And note it duly down.

WON'T WAIT

NIGHT

I am not tired of the stars,
Are you, who have been with us
Since before we were. Likewise
The moon, which lit our way

Before we had one. Some
-times I tire when the sun
Stares and burns itself
Down all over the city, our

Windows melting like eyes
That can't keep grief
Inside. Other times, I imagine

The city going suddenly dark,
No emergency but gentle
Capitulation to what is there.

SMALL WORD

(A sonnet in prose)

"That's a small step for man." Neil Armstrong, according to history.
"That's a small step for a man." Neil Armstrong, according to Neil Armstrong.

If he spoke what he meant and, annoyed, claims he did;

If he chews, swallows, knots, spits and sends it flying;

If "a" vanishes into the box for found articles, which keeps expanding to fit all we go on losing;

If no human ear can detect it or machine be sure it's there

—can memory make history a misquote?

An article vanishes into its vacuum. Does it make a sound?

The other lesson: listen to your mother.

If it matters, enunciate.

If you're wrong, hold your tongue.

DARK SKY

    1.   Held together with duct tape and bungees
Our drone hovers, ticking off the street lights
Lining our cities, which used to lie,
Patient animals, under the night. Now,

They buzz and shimmer, bad news, like us
Full of glitter: hear them always
Humming. Don't measure. Don't stargaze
To find your way: dark space also travels

Between glimmers and maps a continent
Where this idea arose full of vastness
And motion, opening all night. How

Do you track yourself through that -scape
Pin to pinprick, fireplace to fire? Do you
Lose yourself if you can't get lost?

2.   *Get lost*, we say. And can't. We
Build straight boulevards not to, lamp them,
Stand in the foothills admiring the view
We made, five-hundred square miles of heaven

Ordering the void. When we were children,
The sky whelmed overhead, stars so dense
We named the whole grand gesture for milk
Spilling a path. But later, slipping out

After bedtime, we ghosted unlit backyards
Tree to tree, shadow to story, our routes
Defined by darkness. Have we forgotten

The geography of the night, so eager to see
Right where we place our feet? Until
We forget how to find our way.

3.   Forgetting ourselves, now we find our way
With just one sense, not by nerve and skin
Exquisitely tuned, by nose or song, but deep
Inside our heads where image lives, vision's

Push-me-pull-you commandeering what
Little brain we use. We let the rest
Go dark, wrap our feet with leather
And nylon so they can't feel the path

Rising up to meet them, and can't recall
How we once kept our balance by
Losing it, skeletons swaying, suspended

Sole to skull. When was the last time
You felt hair lifting on your arms?
Or tasted air—do you remember?

4.   Taste the air. Remember
Something or someone you can all but
Name moves behind you, becoming
Atmosphere. My ears are plugged in

Half the time to voices coming at me
A continent away, across an ocean,
And wouldn't hear a foot set down
Right next to me. We fear

The thing we can't see, and only that.
As shadows retreat into their corners
We no longer find the need to wonder

What they hide. Or no longer need
Our sense of wander, and forget
Mystery moves us, and the dark within—

    5.   Or misery? To remove the dark within
We illuminate ourselves. I walk down
My front path and a light goes on, mere
Presence switching it, automatic. I wonder

How it sees me, by what particular
Eye. One sensor picks up heartbeat,
Another sees heat. One emits
Rays and waits for their reflection. Bat

-like, my favorite pulses sonar then
Listens for my return. Were I an insect
Flying, it could intercept me, hung

-er swimming down the dark. Except
Our fixture's flightless. I'm no lightning bug,
Just a small body, opening a door—

6.   any small body. Any door ajar.
We're not all that moves. The screech owl
Housing in the maple above our walk trips
Our light all night, all spring. We duct-tape

A camera one birch over, night-adapted,
Feather-triggered. The male lofts across
Our screen with food for mate then chicks:
Grey ghost of worm dangling from his beak,

Ghost of mouse, once or twice a vole,
Limp and heavy. Blinked on when he passes
Light blinds our silent movie, any eye

Using the dark to see. We switch it off. In high
Midsummer daylight, one bright noon
The owlets fledge. And in a week are gone.

7.   The owlets have fledged, here then gone
Then there, who-who-ing out the deeper
Shade of oaks, twitching infrared cameras
Rigged at the back fountain, and we turn our

Backs to the view, close our eyes to recall what
Stars once looked like, overbrimming sky,
Reminding us the way to find by dark. Then,
Distance, brimming in us: do you

Remember your unknowing? Being us,
I guess we need to see. Seeing, we forget
Without the dark no light the universe

Sends us means a thing. Human, up to
Here in meaning, we jury-rig machines. So
Pass the tape and bungees. Hold together.

SPACE

More than one
Surface against which

The physicist
                        sharpens
Herself. I don't mean

To quarrel.
                        Meanwhile,
Light and flurry, wasps

Circle a clearing
Full of sun and where

It comes from.
                        Do not
Think they remain

Unmoved, don't swarm
And sting. We breathe

Motes so tiny we
Don't notice
                        they affix

And wait; we spy
Farther, sending

Machines as if they
Were thoughts
                        to see a way

Beyond. Give them
Room to stretch, matter

Smoothing over whatever
Long term is.
                    So what

We can't see it
                    like
Most of what matters,

Never have or will,
Your lucky stars.

FLY ME

1969

Which is the epic moment? Billowing-off or craft's fly-fall
to surface, huffing flames and dust, all those one

-eyed creatures in enormous skins fumbling down the
ladder. Still carried away a half-century later, they bounce
and drift in gorgeous klutziness, weight and its

-lessness in tense negotiation, stars backdropped against the
dark, oddly endearing. Who would know: inside the suits
they are slimmish, pink, almost hairless by mammalian
standards, too damned smooth. Do they realize how far *out
there* is until they think about getting back?

So, space, what a joke, cold place
harboring monsters, fire, a catch in the throat. Empty
—not empty, whatever they believe,

they do the job: keep sprightly while the
camera runs, slightly comic in their dignity, boys cavorting
(The miracle: not only that they're up there, but through
space and time I can see them at it)

across the surface, trying to keep grounded. Now, they
dance to my command—hit *play*—grainy, black and white

(*man, it looks like the moon or something*),

their extreme high tech old-fashioned now, back

—sliding into the past.

2019

           I admit it: I too wanted to put my foot down,
who didn't? To play the game called *Look at me*,
something to tell the children I would never have,
just as well

Given my mess of space. Blue eye looking askance. From
here, I see a grey face not looking back. If that lump of rock
had a man in it, he might wonder about us, might stop
blowing his horns until I left off gazing to consider

the world through his eyes, something closer to home.
Please sir, can you say cheese?

           Meanwhile, why do I love only from too far
away to reach? Why go anywhere at all, and also why not?

           Meanwhile, since I'm asking, who's driving
this spaceship, tell me who's reading the maps? Not I, joy

-riding through the void, fancy-free, thought

-less, entirely without feck, concerned only with my street

-level destination, burning toward it, skidding right at the corner,
left at the second signal, speeding orb in mind,
what's the point asking where or why, how or even whether
we might ever come to ground. Mean

-while, Happy birthday Lander, you who put down. Happy
birthday, Moon, put upon. For us, oh Earth, idea,
touchstone, vehicle on which time sorts us: help us, won't
you, hold together here?

IN ORBIT

Fall over the horizon
And keep falling, free
As whiplash and moon
Rising on the half-hour. Why

Do I imagine the orbit
Not my own? My shadow
Standing right here,

The northern hemisphere
Cranks a hard end, so
I hope, and tonight's
Snow moon beams never

So lovely, face big as might
Reflect a lost sun dreaming
Winter's last field into being.

DOME WITH STARS

I think to feel better. I need no
Time to prepare. Lying here

On the floor, the problem is

Never enough, too many
Inches and eons. The program

Loads while the house lights

Fade. Stars, then the computer
Glitches and the wiz

Pushing switches says, *ignore*

The horizon, restarts and
The universe fills. Burgeon

And strew fool mind into

Seeing all the way
Where space fires and flames

Out, forgetting all can't be

Twinkle and rapture when
Forever's dark and cold.

SEEING THE BLACK HOLE,

become a stranger. No
Better than absence
Ringed by what arrives.

    Say *the reality*
    Has a face

A long time coming.
Say Einstein was right
Where he didn't

    Want to be, at *too much*
    Matter, its edge absolute

Vanishing. See what
Can't be seen, what can't
Escape itself. May

    Be we could all be
    Tempted; equations have

Been trying to tell us so
Long we always walk off
-kilter ("*what a time*

    To be alive"), only
    Ever meant to fall.

THE NEWS FROM HERE

    1.   What we hear is not
What we know. Where we sit
Makes everything trouble

Or not. Where we stand, not
A jot or tittle can reach
If we don't let it, nothing moves us

Any more or pierces
The glorious iridescent bubble
Of our preoccupations. While

The syllogism (*no news is*
Etc.) doesn't work in reverse
We insist on taking this

As good news, why
Not? Can't we watch

2.   Rome burn down screens
We hold in our palms? What luck
We don't live there, or in

-habit any of those thickets
Or woods we used to visit,
Envying their deepening

Shade and the creatures it hid:
Startled faces and win
-ning habits, whatever did

Become of them? Or the cities
We didn't know we'd sacked
Until we had done, leaving

Children with sooty
Faces, their parents rooting

3.   Dumpsters already emptied
Of our discarded goods. When
Ours, they were all good,

And when tossed still good
Enough for others. Can we be
Blamed we followed the path

Every civilization takes, our golden
Blaze into being merely random
So hardly news; or for the filth

Our fires leave when only
Ashes remain, the wind
Drawing their curtain to hide

Our exit, the stage we abandon
In our aimless, inartful *so long.*

AMAZE

This I want to know
And don't, and how. Also,
What it is. Anything

But gasp, mouth open to let
Pure vowels go. Not by looking
Only: light tells me

How to put my feet but hides
Where I am
Carrying me. The lens shows

What I've never seen and keeps
Me focused. No
Matter, the smallest thing

Or largest I believe to be
Alive I'll later discover
Always watching. Feel

A way: what the instrument sees
Arrives at my eyes too late,
Alight and adrift, to guide me.

THE ROBOT EMANCIPATES ITSELF

In this at least it's way
Ahead of me, sunk in a body

Not too happy with
The way I'm sloping

Along, wires fizzing
And clocks unsorted. Think

Success in circuit
And these automata will make

Art after their makers
Long go, according

To program adapting, becoming
What the artists delighted in

Failing to imagine. Whose
Idea was it? Hard

Not to think about
The Tin Man: a little oil,

A buffing rag, we're
Good to go. Then again

It rained. He needed
Handling as much as any

Ever did. Unlike
Most of us, he knew it.

HIS NEW DREAM

We were driving up a road into, he doesn't know, a wood then a wilderness, and at first he didn't worry but as we climbed the road got steeper and rougher, then steeper still, until at last the car was driving straight up a cliff, nosing the air. The engine strained and the car bucked, threatening to tumble headlights-over-trunk down the mountain. He wanted to stop, he says, but we kept on.

I ask, *Did we make it?*

We did, he says, as if this isn't the point. *Barely.*

As an afterthought, I ask, *Who was driving?*

You were, he says. *It was your car.*

DREAM TRIGGER

I am packed into sleep like feathers,
Packed like a gun. In sleep

I have over my shoulder a moon
I see only in the shadow

My body curls around and holds.
My body packs along

What I always have: nothing
But a body and a trigger,

The moon and my shadow
Fluttering like a feather or a flame.

—PHILIA

Biblio-, nebulo-, bee
Afficionado, I go for dairy

And really good sneakers
Lifting me in style. I love to think

I love to think. Since I don't
Love machines for their

Own sake, I am no
Techno-, but a chainsaw

Chewing things over, doing
What it's meant to as well

As anything could, makes me
Laugh out loud. And my heart

In the right place or a pulse
clutched in my fist fills

Itself with and loves
Itself. I am in love really with

The whole shebang: mine,
Sure, but especially yours.

MARS ATTACKS,

my friend calls his book,
And I read not noun/verb

But adjective/noun, not US
Bombs Baghdad but panic

Attacks, heart attacks, attacks
The conscience makes when I

Least expect it. For a full year
I believe my friend is under

Psychic assault. But it's
Movie time after all, flying

And syntax undoing us
Like it always did.

DOWN

Where everything ends up. I lose
Some small gadget from a pocket
And check there, hoping I remembered
Not to flush. It's the responsible

Thing to do, letting things ripen
And collect. Or collect, then
Ripen. This is how the peripheral
Grabs my attention away from that

To which I should devote myself:
My job, say; what's happening with all
Those presidents of Venezuela; who said what
About it. All those things I do nothing

About. The way an empire falls.
Or keeps, as they will, staggering along.

PLATONIC

What can we get behind, if not the
World we see. Made visible

By daylight, under eyelids it may be
All-encompassing or only

A sometimes-lovely backdrop, hell
-uva distraction, temporary place-

holder of presence. Why holster
The mind's lady-pistols? Some days, I'm for

Brandishing purse-sized guns or reality
(*Boom-boom*) sounding like desire.

OVERHEARD

Before I got married, I slept in the buff.
I don't know if Z knows this, or if
He ever did. I cannot tell R
From V on the keyboard. I should

Be prone to collapse. I felt it
Might have been more prudent for S
Not to have said all he did, whatever occurs
Where matter and time blink. If I'd

Waited for perfection I'd be out cold,
Another moonshot. It's a cliché to call
Life a journey, tilt-a-whirl, bad
Idea, a fat old fireworks show, a statistical

Fluctuation, anything at all. Cherry pie,
I've never liked it. A la mode.

ABIDE

I would like a blue
House with gold highlights
The dream says to me.

The dream would like
A house in which to instruct me
What architecture is, what

Is light. Any dream
Would be happy to be
This one, blue and gold

And brimful of words
As mine is. So
Would I. So would I.

POET AND POEM

Can you tell
One from the other? Made
Of the same old words
Each reflects itself

And one the other. Made
More, the poem elaborates
Its reflection; the poem
Fills with substance, a form

Becoming more. Ornamented
Or not, maybe the poet's
Full of herself, body being
What the poem may miss.

Or not. Maybe the poem's
Everything the poet isn't
Missing, or the poem may be
How you face the poet

With all she's not.
Minding her portrait, the painter
Faces off the poet
And the poem, realizing

A portrait reminds; the paint
Uncovers something new.
The painting realizes
The poet and the pose

It reveals, something new
Out of the same old words.
Maybe the pose is real.
How do you tell?

NICO, FOUR MONTHS

Already looking outward, this person
Faces the world squarely
And takes it all in the way she does.
Under her sailor hat, she sports

Stripes. Someone likes them, possibly
Not her. Who knows what fripperies
She will choose? Will there be creepers
With rumple soles and spangles, high- or low-

Tops, a fascinator? Can this person,
Tucked deep in a tiny NASA spacesuit, say
Genius? Already long in gaze. With this

Person, whatever's up? So far none
Of us can tell. Discuss
It all night long: nobody knows.

LATER

My feet became agnostic. Believed a god
But not in god's existence. Found a path
I didn't take, a star I failed to follow
Home, away. If in daylight I believed

I saw the moon. If the valley lay
Down its dusty floor, all day clouds
Pulled swift shadows across it. I mean
Signs may or may not have flashed

Neon in the north; the south may
Have blown its cyclones to my doorstep,
Bluster after bluster. It was fall,

Wasn't it? And then came winter. It all
Looked like the world. It seemed
Like all the home I'd ever get.

WON'T WAIT

Keep assuming permanence
While everything passes
Faster. Tomorrow only
Traveling, moving places

And skies. Having attained
An age I wouldn't have
Imagined, like any to come,
I don a frock light as air, sky

And bright woods swirling
Pleats around me to wrap
Like a shawl, a hood. So many
Escapes. I once fell in love

Because someone's poem
Filled my head with light, who
Failed to notice the poem turning
Me away, me following, becoming

A corridor going dark. Even
So, thank you, poem. Thank you,
Light. Thank you, time, how
You keep and carry us away.

NOTES

Page 15: The quoted line is from William Carlos Williams.

Page 25: Hung Liu, National Museum of Women's Art, June 2018.

Page 28: For Tom Stillinger.

Page 32: Titled with and after a line from Lee Briccetti, and for her.

Page 34: For biologist Phyllis Coley, with thanks.

Page 60: Dr. Doris Taylor, Texas Heart Institute, Regenerative Medicine Research labs.

Page 61: Mary Ruefle. *When you become invisible, you become your inner life.*

Page 62: For my mother and husband.

Page 69: For W.S. Merwin.

Page 70: For Wendy Battin.

Page 84: https://www.space.com/17307-neil-armstrong-one-small-step-quote.html

Page 85: The Keck Drone, assembled as described, flies city streets at night and measures artificial light. It is part of the Dark Sky Project at the University of Utah, which has assembled a diverse group of scholars and experts from the sciences, arts, humanities, and other fields to research and find solutions to light pollution.

Page 97: Thanks for the private show to the Hayden Planetarium at the American Museum of Natural History.

Page 98: "Black Hole Picture Revealed for the First Time," *New York Times*, April 10, 2019. The italicized lines are from the article; the quoted lines were spoken by cosmologist Janna Levin.

Page 103: Title from *Robots and Artists*, Grand Palace, 2018.

Page 107: After a title by Wyn Cooper, and for him.

Page 109: Richard Powers: *The visible is only a placeholder for real desire.*

Page 112: After a painting by Maureen O'Hara Ure.

ACKNOWLEDGMENTS

Poems from this collection have appeared in the following journals and magazines:

Ascent: "Dome with Stars," "Fly Me," "Long View," "Noisy Birds," "Whale Fall"; *Battery Journal*: "Breasts," "The News from Here"; *Blackbird*: "Elegy"; *DIAGRAM*: "Platonic," "The Robot Emancipates Itself"; *Gargoyle*: "Invisible," "Magnolia," "Uncanny"; *Hudson Review*: "If the Older I Get the Less I Know—"; *Ocean State Review*: "—Philia"; *Seneca Review*: "Seven (or so) Poses"; *Sugarhouse Review*: "Sick of Grief—" (as "Sick of people's grief"); Terrain.org: "Animal," "Bird," "Worm"; *The Fourth River*: "Bee," "Pelican Takes My Hand"; *upstreet*: "Ghost Apples," "If the Mind Fears Freedom," "Small Song."

"You Won't Find Consolation" was first published as a "Poem of the Day" on Poets.org, selected by Paisley Rekdal.

"Tilt" was commissioned for *Poetry and Place*, an exhibition of poems alongside works by artist Dianne Firth. Belconnen Art Centre Canberra, Australia, August 25–September 17, 2017.

"The News from Here" was commissioned for *No News: 90 Poets Reflect on a Unique BBC Newscast* (Canberra: Recent Work Press, 2020).

"Fly Me" was commissioned for *Giant Steps*, eds. Shane Strange and Paul Munden. (Canberra: Recent Work Press, 2019).

"Dark Sky" was commissioned for "Women, Poetry, Science: Celebrating the Amazing," *Axon: Creative Explorations*, vol. 9, no. 2 (Summer 2019).

BIOGRAPHICAL NOTE

Katharine Coles' eleven books include *Wayward*, poems from Red Hen Press; a memoir, *Look Both Ways*; and a collection of essays, *The Stranger I Become: on Walking, Looking, and Writing*. 2018–19 Poet-in-Residence at the Natural History Museum of Utah and the Salt Lake Public Library for the Poets House FIELD WORK program, she has received awards from the National Endowment for the Arts, the National Endowment for the Humanities, and the National Science Foundation's Antarctic Artists and Writers Program, and from the Guggenheim Foundation. She is a Distinguished Professor at the University of Utah.

CPSIA information can be obtained
at www.ICGtesting.com
Printed in the USA
LVHW030803130323
741471LV00002B/2